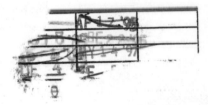

FORTY POEMS
TOUCHING ON
RECENT AMERICAN
HISTORY

edited by
ROBERT BLY

BEACON PRESS   BOSTON

CONTENTS

TO THE STATES

THE DICTATORSHIP OF THE FLIES

RECENT WARS

THE PEOPLE

ORIGINALS OF THE POEMS IN SPANISH AND GERMAN

Leaping Up Into Political Poetry

1

POEMS touching on American history are clearly
political poems. Most educated people advise that
poetry on political subjects should not be attempted.
For an intricate painting, we are urged to bring
forward our finest awareness. At the same time, we
understand that we should leave that awareness
behind when we go to examine political acts. Our
wise men and wise institutions assure us that
national political events are beyond the reach of
ordinary, or even extraordinary, human sensitivity.

That habit is not new: Thoreau's friends thought
that his writings on nature were very good, but that
he was beyond his depth when he protested against
the Mexican War. The circumstances surrounding
the Austrian Franz Jagerstätter, whose life ended
thirty years ago, during the Second World War, are
very interesting in this connection. Jagerstätter was
a farmer, with the equivalent of a high school educa-
tion, though he possessed a remarkable intelligence.
He decided that the Nazis were incompatible with
the best he had seen or read of life, and made this
decision before the Nazis took over in Austria; he
cast the only "no" ballot in his village against the
Anschluss. Jagerstätter's firm opposition to the Nazi
regime is particularly interesting because he did not
act out a doctrinaire position of a closely knit group,
like the Jehovah's Witnesses, nor was he a member
of a group being systematically wiped out, like the
Jews: he simply made up his mind on a specific
political situation, relying on his own judgment, and
what he was able to piece together from the Bible,
and using information available to everyone.

When drafted by the Nazis after the Anschluss, he refused to serve. The military judges sympathized, but told him they would have to cut off his head if he did not change his mind. Gordon Zahn's book, *In Solitary Witness*, recounts the meetings Jägerstätter had with various authorities shortly before his execution. All persons in authority who interviewed Jägerstätter, including bishops of the Austrian Catholic Church, psychiatrists, lawyers, and judges, told him that his sensibility was advising him wrongly. He was not responsible for acts he might take as a soldier: that was the responsibility of the legal government. They told him that he should turn his sensibility to the precarious situation of his family. He was advised, in effect, not to be serious. It was recommended that he be Christian in regard to his domestic life, but not to his political life. By study Jägerstätter had increased the range of his sensibility, and now this sensibility looked on acts he would have to take under orders by the government with the same calm penetration with which it would look on wasting time, or deciding on the quality of a book. He had extended his awareness farther than society wanted him to, and everyone he met, with the exception of a single parish priest, tried to drive it back again. Jägerstätter, however, refused to change his mind, would not enter the army despite disturbed appeals by the authorities, and was executed.

Most Americans have serious doubts about the morality of the Vietnam War. We are all aware of the large number of spirited and courageous young Americans in the Resistance who are refusing induction and are risking and being given lengthy prison sentences.

The majority of American draftees, however, go into the Army as they are told. Their doubt is interrupted on its way, and does not continue forward to end in an act, as Jagerstatter's doubt did or as the objector's and resister's doubt does. This failure to carry through means essentially that American culture has succeeded in killing some sensibilities. In order to take the rebellious and responsible action, the man thinking must be able to establish firm reasons for it; and in order to imagine those reasons, his awareness must have grown, over years, finer and finer. The "invisible organs of government," schools, broadcasting houses, orthodox churches, move to kill the awareness. The schools emphasize competitiveness over compassion; television and advertising do their part in numbing the sensibilities. Killing awareness is easier than killing the man later for a firm act.

2

The calculated effort of a society to kill awareness helps explain why so few citizens take rebellious actions. But I'm not sure it explains why so few American poets have written political poems. A poem can be a political act, but it has not been so far at least an illegal act. Moreover, since much of the poet's energy goes toward extending his awareness, he is immune to the more gross effects of brainwashing. Why then have so few American poems penetrated to any reality in our political life? I think one reason is that political concerns and inward concerns have always been regarded in our tradition as opposites, even incompatibles. *Time* is very upset that Buddhists should take part in political activity: the *Time* writers are convinced that the worlds are two mutually exclusive worlds, and if you work in one, you are excused from working in the other. English and American poets have adopted this schemata also, and poets in the Fifties felt that in *not* writing anything political, they were doing something meritorious. It's clear that many of the events that create our foreign relations and our domestic relations come from more or less hidden impulses in the American psyche. It's also clear I think that some sort of husk has grown around that psyche, so that in the Fifties we could not look into it or did not. The Negroes and the Vietnam War have worn the husk thin in a couple of places now. But if that is so, then the poet's main job is to penetrate that husk around the American psyche, and since that psyche is inside *him* too, the writing of political poetry is like the writing of personal poetry, a sudden drive by the poet inward.

As a matter of fact, we notice that it has been inward poets, Robert Duncan, Denise Levertov, and Galway Kinnell, who have written the best poems about the Vietnam War.

When a poet succeeds in driving part way inward, he often develops new energy that carries him on through the polished husk of the inner psyche that deflects most citizens or poets. Once inside the psyche, he can speak of inward and political things with the same assurance. We can make a statement then that would not have been accepted in the Thirties, namely, that what is needed to write good poems about the outward world is inwardness. The political activists in the literary world are wrong—they try to force political poetry out of poets by pushing them more deeply into events, making them feel guilt if they don't

10

abandon privacy. But the truth is that the political poem comes out of the deepest privacy.

3

Let me continue a minute with the comparison of the political poem with the personal poem. I'll use Yeat's marvellous word *entangle*; he suggested that the symbolist poem entangles some substance from the divine world in its words. Similarly a great personal poet like Villon entangles some of the private substance of his life in his language so well that hundreds of years later it still remains embedded. The subject of personal poetry is often spiritual growth, or the absence of it.

The dominant poem in American literature has always been the personal poem. John Crowe Ransom, for instance, wrote an elegant version of the personal poem, Randall Jarrell a flabby version, Robert Lowell a harsh version, Reed Whittemore a funny version, W. D. Snodgrass a whining version, and Robert Creeley a laconic one, etc. I love the work of many of these poets, but they choose, on the whole, not to go beyond the boundaries of the personal poem. Many poets say flatly—and proudly —that they are "not political." If a tree said that, I would find it more convincing than when a man says it. I think it is conceivable that a tree could report that it grew just as well in the Johnson administration as in the Kennedy administration or the Lincoln administration. But a modern man's spiritual life and his growth are increasingly sensitive to the tone and content of a regime. A man of draft age will find that his life itself depends on the political content of an administration. So these poets' assertion of independence, I think, is a fiction.

The only body of political poetry written with any determination in the U.S. were those written during the Thirties by Edwin Rolfe, Sol Funaroff, Kenneth Fearing, among others. It is interesting that their poems were usually political in *opinions*. For example, the poet might declare that he had discovered who the phonies in the world are, something he didn't know before. But changes of opinion are steps in the growth of the poet's personality, they are events in his psychic history. These "political" poems of the Thirties then were not really political poems at all, but personal poems appearing under another guise.

We find many political poems composed entirely of opinions; they are political but not poems. Here is an example from a Scandinavian anthology:

> Poor America
> so huge, so strong, so afraid.
> afraid in Guatamala,
> afraid in Congo, Panama,
> afraid in Cuba, in Santo Domingo,
> afraid in Vietnam . . .
> America, take your hands off Vietnam!
> The poor are rising
> You are through stealing now
> Your face is distorted with hate . . .

These lines have boiled off the outermost layer of the brain. The poem is not inside the poet's own life, let alone inside this nation's life.

The life of the nation can be imagined also not as something deep inside our psyche, but as a psyche larger than the psyche of anyone living, a larger sphere, floating above everyone. In order

12

for the poet to write a true political poem, he has to be able to have such a grasp of his own concerns that he can leave them for a while, and then leap up into this other psyche. He wanders about there a while, and as he returns he brings back plant-seeds that have stuck to his clothes, some inhabitants of this curious sphere, which he then tries to keep alive with his own psychic body.

Some poets try to write political poems impelled by hatred, or fear. But these emotions are heavy, they affect the gravity of the body. What the poet needs to get up that far and bring back something are great leaps of the imagination.

A true political poem is a quarrel with ourselves, and the rhetoric is as harmful in that sort of poem as in the personal poem. The true political poem does not order us either to take any specific acts: like the personal poem, it moves to deepen awareness.

Thinking of the rarity of the political poem in the United States, another image comes to mind. We can imagine Americans inside a sphere, like those sad men in Bosch's "Garden of Earthly Delights." The clear glass is the limit of the ego. We float inside it. Around us there are worlds of energy, but we are unable to describe them in words, because we are unable to get out of our own egos.

4

The political poem needs an especially fragrant language. Neruda's "The Dictators" has that curious fragrance that comes from its words brushing unknown parts of the psyche. It seems to me a masterpiece of the political poem :

An odor has remained among the sugar cane:

13

A mixture of blood and body, a penetrating
Petal that brings nausea.
Between the coconut palms the graves are full
Of ruined bones, of speechless death-rattles.
A delicate underling converses
With glasses, braid collars, and cords of gold.
The tiny palace gleams like a watch
And the rapid laughs with gloves on
Cross the corridors at times
And join the dead voices
And the blue mouths freshly buried.
The weeping is hidden like a water-plant
Whose seeds fall constantly on the earth
And without light make the great blind leaves to
    grow.
Hatred has grown scale upon scale,
Blow on blow, in the ghastly water of the swamp,
With a snout full of ooze and silence.

The poem's task is to entangle in the language
the psychic substance of a South American country
under a dictator. The Spanish original, of course, is
much more resonant. But even in the translation it
is clear that Neruda is bringing in unexpected
images: " The tiny palace gleams like a watch "—
images one would expect in an entirely different
sort of poem: " rapid laughs with gloves on." Sud-
denly a blind plant appears, that reproduces itself
by dropping seeds constantly on the ground, shaded
by its own huge leaves. This image is complicated,
created by a part of the mind inaccessible to hatred,
and yet it carries the reality of hatred radiating
from dictators into the consciousness with a kind of
massive intelligence.

Describing dictators in " The United Fruit Com-
pany," Neruda uses for them the image of ordinary

14

houseflies. By contrast, the journalistic mind would tend to describe them as huge and cunning. Whitman was the first true political poet we had in North America. His short poem "To The States," with which this book opens, has great fragrance in its language as well. "(With gathering murk, with muttering thunder and lambent shoots we all duly awake)".

William Vaughn Moody in 1898 wrote some powerful lines :

> Are we the eagle nation Milton saw
> Mewing its mighty youth,
> Soon to possess the mountain winds of truth,
> And be swift familiar of the sun
> Where aye before God's face his trumpets run?
> Or have we but the talons and the maw,
> And for the abject likeness of our heart
> Shall some less lordly bird be set apart?
> Some gross-billed wader where the swamps are
> fat?
> Some gorger in the sun? Some prowler with the
> bat?

His poem was written against United States policy the first time we invaded Cuba. The language at times is remarkably swift and intense, particularly when compared to the hopelessly foggy language of political poetry being written by others at that time.

The political poem in the U.S. after Whitman and Moody lay dormant until the inventive generation of 1917 came along. It revived with mixed results. Pound demanded that American history enter his Cantos, Eliot wrote well, though always of a generalized modern nation, rather than of the U.S.; Jeffers wrote marvellously, but really was not interested in the U.S. as a nation at all. In the next generation,

15

Cummings wrote of this country using a sense of superiority as his impulse; he almost never escaped from himself. After Cummings the New Critical mentality, profoundly opposed to any questioning of the white power structure, took over, and the language and strength of political poetry survived only in three men, in Kenneth Rexroth, Thomas McGrath, and a slightly younger man, David Ignatow. During the Forties and Fifties most poets kept away from the political poem. In his "Ode For The American Dead in Korea," Thomas McGrath wrote :

And God (whose sparrows fall aslant his gaze,
Like grace or confetti) blinks, and he is gone,
And you are gone . . . But, in another year
We will mourn you, whose fossil courage fills
The limestone histories: brave: ignorant: amazed:
Dead in the rice paddies, dead on the nameless
    hills.

Rexroth has written beautiful political poems, among them "A Christmas Note For Geraldine Udell." his great common sense and stubborn intelligence helped immensely in keeping the political poem alive.

The new critical influence in poetry began to dim in the middle 1950's, just at the time American's fantastic capacity for aggression and self-delusion began to be palpable like rising water to the beach walker. William Carlos Williams' refusal to ignore political lies was passed on to Allen Ginsberg; Neruda's example began to take hold; Rexroth, McGrath and Ignatow continued to write well; Ferlinghetti separately wrote his "A Tentative Description Of A Dinner Given To Promote The Impeachment of President Eisenhower." Many black poets began to be visible. As the Vietnam war escalated, Robert Duncan wrote several powerful poems on the War. His "Uprising" ends:

> this specter that in the beginning Adams and
>   Jefferson feared and knew
> would corrupt the very body of the nation
>   and all our sense of our common humanity . .
> now shines from the eyes of the President
>   in the swollen head of the nation.

I have not included that poem here, nor many other poems that have been written during the Vietnam War; they, or a selection of them, are printed in *A Poetry Reading Against The Vietnam War*, which really begins where this book leaves off.

5

For this anthology of poems touching on recent American history, I have chosen the poems that I thought penetrated most deeply into the psyche of the nation, not caring whether the poet was of the right or the left. I am interested not only in the political poem as an imaginative form, but also in the picture of the United States that comes out of these poems. Having just a few pages, I have left out some poems of Cummings, Jeffers, and Williams known to us from anthologies, preferring to use the space for poems by younger poets.

America is still young herself, and she may become something magnificent and shining, or she may turn, as Rome did, into a black dinosaur, the enemy of every nation in the world who wants to live its own life. In my opinion, that decision has not yet been made.

—ROBERT BLY

" You can no more have the greatest poetry without a nation than religion without symbols. One can only reach out to the universe with a gloved hand—that glove is one's nation, the only thing one knows even a little of."

YEATS

To The States

TO THE STATES

To Identify the 16th, 17th, or 18th Presidentiad

Why reclining, interrogating ? why myself and all
    drowsing ?
What deepening twilight—scum floating atop of the
    waters,
Who are they as bats and night-dogs askant in the
    capitol ?
What a filthy Presidentiad ! (O South, your torrid
    suns ! O North, your arctic freezings !)
Are those really Congressmen; are those the great
    Judges ? is that the President ?
Then I will sleep awhile yet, for I see that these States
    sleep, for reasons;
(With gathering murk, with muttering thunder and
    lambent shoots we all duly awake,
South, North, East, West, inland and seaboard, we
    will surely awake).

WALT WHITMAN

" IOWA, KANSAS, NEBRASKA "

Iowa, Kansas, Nebraska,
all combustible country
under a tortured sky.
Nothing ever happens here
except loneliness;
wheatfields squirming in the sun,
the plains dry as biscuits.

Yet the people grow.

In the Oklahoma air
oil is prince of blossoms;
Texas is the Kingdom.

Fortune's richest man
plays croquet in Dallas.
He is seventy,
afraid of centipedes,
hesitates at watery places,
for a gypsy slipped him once
the dark blue ace of drowning,
never kissed a woman
(nor a man either),
likes to ride his zebra
several times each morning
round his private race-track,
bought the Lone Star his third
year collecting our planet,
later added forty-
seven others: stars, white,
plays croquet in Dallas
at four o'clock in starlight.

Yet, somehow, the people grow.

GENE FRUMKIN

22

EISENHOWER'S VISIT TO FRANCO, 1959

". . . we die of cold, and not of darkness."

UNAMUNO

The American hero must triumph over
The forces of darkness.
He has flown through the very light of heaven
And come down in the slow dusk
Of Spain.

Franco stands in a shining circle of police,
His arms open in welcome.
He promises all dark things
Will be hunted down

Meanwhile,
State police yawn in the prisons,
Antonio Machado follows the moon
Down a road of white dust,
To a cave of silent children
Under the Pyrenees.
Wine darkens in stone jars in villages.
Wine sleeps in the mouth of old men, It is a dark
        red color.

Smiles glitter in Madrid.
Eisenhower has touched hands with Franco,
        embracing
In a glare of photographers.
Clean new bombers from America muffle their
        engines
And glide down now.
Their wings shine in the search-lights
Of bare fields,
In Spain.

JAMES WRIGHT

HOW COME?

I'm in New York covered by a layer of soap foam.
The air is dense from the top of skyscrapers
to the sidewalk in every street, avenue
and alley, as far as Babylon on the East,
Dobbs Ferry on the North, Coney Island
on the South and stretching far over
the Atlantic Ocean. I wade
through, breathing by pushing
foam aside. The going is slow,
with just a clearing ahead
by swinging my arms. Others are groping
from all sides, too. We keep moving.
Everything else has happened here
and we've survived: snow storms,
traffic tieups, train breakdowns, bursting
water mains; and now I am writing
with a lump of charcoal stuck between my toes,
switching it from one foot to the other—
this monkey trick learned visiting
with my children at the zoo of a Sunday.
But soap foam filling the air,
the bitter, fatty smell of it . . . How come?
My portable says it extends to San Francisco!
Listen to this, and down to the Mexican border
and as far north as Canada. All the prairies,
the Rocky Mountains, the Great Lakes, Chicago,
the Pacific Coast. No advertising stunt
could do this. The soap has welled out of the ground
says the portable suddenly. The scientists report
the soil saturated. And now what?
We'll have to start climbing for air,
a crowd forming around the Empire State Building
says the portable. God help the many
who will die of soap foam.

DAVID IGNATOW

24

I KNOW A MAN

As I sd to my
friend, because I am
always talking, — John, I

sd, which was not his
name, the darkness sur-
rounds us, what

can we do against
it, or else, shall we &
why not, buy a goddamn big car,

drive, he sd, for
christ's sake, look
out where yr going.

ROBERT CREELEY

IN THE OREGON COUNTRY

From old Fort Walla Walla and the Klickitats
to Umpqua near Port Orford, stinking fish tribes
massacred our founders, the thieving whites.

Chief Rotten Belly slew them at a feast;
Kamiakin riled the Snakes and Yakimas;
all spurted arrows through the Cascades west.

Those tribes became debris on their own lands:
Captain Jack's wide face above the rope,
His Modoc women dead with twitching hands.

The last and most splendid, Nez Perce
Chief Joseph, fluttering eagles through Idaho,
dashed his pony-killing getaway.

They got him. Repeating rifles bored at his head,
and in one fell look Chief Joseph saw the game
out of that spiral mirror all explode.

Back of the Northwest map their country goes,
mountains yielding and hiding fold on fold,
gorged with yew trees that were good for bows.

WILLIAM STAFFORD

from CANTO 89

Commander Rogers observed that the sea was
    sprinkled with fragments of West India fruit
and followed that vestige.
    Giles talked and listened,
more listened and did not read.
    Young Jessie did not forward dispatches
so Fremont proceeded toward the North West and
    we ultimately embraced Californy.
The Collingwood manned 80 guns.
    "Those who wish to talk
May leave now" said Rossini,
    "Madame Bileau is going to play."
" Trade,
    trade,
        trade ! "
            Sang Lanier.
Van Buren already in '37 unsmearing Talleyrand.
And the elderly Aida, then a girl of 16, in the '90 s,
    visiting some very stiff friends in New England
giggled (and thereby provoked sour expressions)
    when some children crossed the front lawn
        with
a bottle of water strung on a string between them
    and chanting:
        " Martin
Van Buren, a bottle of urine."
        Sagetrieb, or the
oral tradition.

" Ten men," said Ubaldo, "who will charge a nest of
    machine guns
    for one who will put his name on chit."

        EZRA POUND

A WARNING TO ABRAHAM LINCOLN

Captain, I have seen
the tranquil honey bees fly out
from the hollow socket of your wound
and light down in the eyes of Walt Whitman
and make his reverberating beard seem alive.

I am looking for you, Captain,
because I have heard that they would love to kill you
        once more.
This time we know it.

Don't you hear the footsteps outside
of the man who is conspiring among the grass-
        hoppers,
setting loose the swarm, and already enjoying the
        gorging of green things?

Careful, Captain, careful.
The wheat heads are nervous, and the sky is somber.
Elytrons and pincers and mandibles
are warning you: careful.

Up there, in your box.

I know of it, and so I am warning you,
because the light is being shut out above the finest
        fields.
And not one stone will remain on another,
because your city is already crying through its
        window chinks.

If they do kill you once more,
who will harvest the honey from your hives,
or guide your nourishing peace
through the tunnels to your ants ?

If they do kill you once more,
who will take care of your black ants ?
If they do kill you once more,
your careful watch over the anthills
from sunrise until dark
will never be possible again,
not even in the laurel leaves of sleep.

I am looking for you, Captain,
to say that they are looking for you
with the muzzle of a revolver
which would like to open a fresh wound without bees,
because in that hollow place of your death without
        blood
all your hives would die.

And where
are we going to bury you this time,
we who walk toward your voice like a bee's,
and drink from your sad eyes ?

Is there a place
where you won't
be alive any more, but dead ?

JACINTO FOMBONA-PACHANO
translated by Robert Bly

THE DICTATORSHIP OF THE FLIES

ON AMERICAN ISLAND WARS

I

Alas ! what sounds are these that come
Sullenly over the Pacific seas, —
Sounds of ignoble battle, striking dumb
The season's half-awakened ecstasies ?
Must I be humble, then,
Now when my heart hath need of pride ? . . . .
Too sorely heavy is the debt they lay
On me and the companions of my day.
I would remember now
My country's goodliness, make sweet her name.
Alas ! what shade art thou
Of sorrow or of blame
Liftest the lyric leafage from her brow,
And pointest a slow finger at her shame ?

II

Lies ! Lies ! It cannot be ! The wars we wage
Are noble, and our battles still are won
By justice for us, ere we lift the gage.
We have not sold our loftiest heritage.
The proud republic hath not stooped to cheat
And scramble in the market-place of war;
Her forehead weareth yet its solemn star.
Here is her witness this, her perfect son,
This delicate and proud New England soul
Who leads despiséd men, with just-unshackled feet,
Up the large ways where death and glory meet,

33

To show all peoples that our shame is done,
That once more we are clean and spirit-whole.

III

Though furtively the sunlight seems to grieve,
And the spring-laden breeze
Out of the gladdening west is sinister
With sounds of nameless battle overseas;
Though when we turn the question in suspense
If these things be indeed after these ways,
And what things are to follow after these,
Our fluent men of place and consequence
Fumble and fill their mouths with hollow phrase,
Or for the end-all of deep arguments
Intone their dull commercial liturgies—
I dare not yet believe ! My ears are shut !
I will not hear the thin satiric praise
And muffled laughter of our enemies,
Bidding us never sheathe our valiant sword
Till we have changed our birthright for a gourd
Of wild pulse stolen from a barbarian's hut;
Showing how wise it is to cast away
The symbols of our spiritual sway,
That so our hands with better ease
May wield the driver's whip and grasp the jailer's
    keys.

IV

Was it for this our fathers kept the law ?
This crown shall crown their struggle and their ruth?
Are we the eagle nation Milton saw
Mewing its mighty youth,

34

Soon to possess the mountain winds of truth,
And be a swift familiar of the sun
Where aye before God's face his trumpets run ?
Or have we but the talons and the maw,
And for the abject likeness of our heart
Shall some less lordly bird be set apart ?
Some gross-billed wader where the swamps are fat?
Some gorger in the sun? Some prowler with the bat ?

WILLIAM VAUGHN MOODY
from *An Ode In Time Of Hesitation*

IMPERATOR VICTUS

Big guns again
No speakee well
But plain.

Again, again —
And they shall tell
The Spanish Main

The Dollar from the Cross.

Big guns again.
But peace to thee,
Andean brain.

That defunct boss.

Big guns again,
Atahualpa,
Imperator Inca —

Slain.

HART CRANE

TO THEODORE ROOSEVELT

1904

Hunter, the only way to approach you
is with a voice like that of the Bible, or poems like
      those of Walt Whitman.
Archaic and modern, simple and involved,
with something of Washington, and more of Nimrod.
In fact you are the United States,
you are the future invader
of the naive America that still has native blood,
that still prays to Jesus Christ, and still speaks
      Spanish.
You are a magnificent and powerful example of your
      race:
you are cultivated; you are efficient, you disagree
Dominating horses or murdering tigers,
      with Tolstoy.
you are an Alexander-Nebuchadnezzar.
(You are a professor of energy,
as the sports would say today.)

You believe that to live is to burn,
that progress is explosion,
that where you place the rifle slug
you place the future.
                  No.
The United States is powerful and great.
When the States shiver a deep shudder
Moves down the enormous vertebrate of the Andes.
If you shout, we hear it like a lion's roar.
Hugo once said to Grant: "You own the stars."
(Hardly visible, the Argentine sun is just rising,
and the star of Chile ascending . . .) You are rich.

You mingle the religion of Hercules with the religion
     of Mammon;
lighting up the road of easy domination of others,
Liberty raises her torch in New York.

But in the America we have, which has produced
     poets
since the ancient days of Netzahualcoyotl,
which has kept the footprints of the great Bacchus,
which even knew at one time the words of Pan,
which used to speak with the stars, which had
     legends of Atlantis,
whose name arrives to us, resonating, in Plato,
which since the most distant beginnings of its life,
lives out of light, out of fire, out of perfume, out of
     love,
America of the great Montezuma, of the Inca,
the odorous America of Christopher Columbus,
Catholic America, Spanish America,
America in which the aristocratic Guatemoc said:
" I do not find myself in a bed of roses "; that America
which is shaken by hurricanes and brought alive by
     love:
Men with Anglo-Saxon eyes and barbaric souls: that
     America is alive,
And it sleeps, and loves, and moves, and is the
     daughter of the Sun.
Be careful. Spanish America is alive!
The Spanish lion has wild cubs around.
Roosevelt, in order to take us in your iron claws
you would have to have been sent by God himself
as the terrifying Rifleman and the mighty Hunter.
It's all arranged, just one thing is missing : God !

RUBEN DARIO
translated by Robert Bly

38

THE UNITED FRUIT CO.

When the trumpet sounded, it was
all prepared on the earth,
and Jehovah parcelled out the earth
to Coca Cola, Inc., Anaconda,
Ford Motors, and other entities:
The Fruit Company, Inc.
reserved for itself the most succulent,
the central coast of my own nation,
the delicate waist of America.
It rechristened its territories
as " The Banana Republic "
and over the dead who were sleeping,
over the restless heroes
who had conquered the magnificence,
over the liberty and the flags,
it established the comic opera:
carried away the free will,
presented crowns of Caesar,
unsheathed envy, attracted
the dictatorship of the flies,
Trujillo flies, Tachos flies,
Carias flies, Martinez flies,
Ubico flies, damp flies
of modest blood and marmalade,
drunken flies who zoom
over the popular graves,
circus flies, wise flies
well trained in tyranny.
Among the blood-thirsty flies
the Fruit Company unloads its ships,
filling up with coffee and with fruit,

in its ships which slip away
as though on dishes, the treasure
of our submerged territories.

Meanwhile into the sugared
chasms of the harbors,
Indians were falling, wrapped
for burial in the mist of the dawn:
a body rolls, a thing
that has no name, a fallen cipher,
a cluster of dead fruit
thrown down on the dump.

PABLO NERUDA
translated by Robert Bly

THE DICTATORS

An odor has remained among the sugar cane:
a mixture of blood and body, a penetrating
petal that brings nausea.
Between the coconut palms the graves are full
of ruined bones, of speechless death-rattles.
A delicate underling converses
with glasses, braid collars, and cords of gold.
The tiny palace gleams like a watch
and the rapid laughs with gloves on
cross the corridors at times
and join the dead voices
and the blue mouths freshly buried.
The weeping is hidden like a water-plant
whose seeds fall constantly on the earth
and without light make the great blind leaves grow.
Hatred has grown scale upon scale,
blow on blow, in the ghastly water of the swamp,
with a snout full of ooze and silence.

PABLO NERUDA
translated by Robert Bly

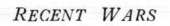

RECENT WARS

THE ODOR OF BLOOD

Odor of blood excites
The violent, powerless dead —
Compelled again and again
To the place of their suicide,

Or haunted by the house
Where forgotten murder was done,
They grow drunk on the smell of the past
As if on the fumes of wine.

So, summoned in sleep
From his civilian dream,
The buried soldier returns
To the scene of an old crime

Where innocence and blood
Were spilled in the ditch of war —
Compelled again and again
By fury of desire

Or memory, to return:
Ghosts weak, bloodthirsty, mad:
As ghost planes tirelessly orbit
The closed fields of the dead.

THOMAS McGRATH

CARENTAN O CARENTAN

Trees in the old days used to stand
And shape a shady lane
Where lovers wandered hand in hand
Who came from Carentan.

This was the shining green canal
Where we came two by two
Walking at combat-interval.
Such trees we never knew.

The day was early June, the ground
Was soft and bright with dew.
Far away the guns did sound,
But here the sky was blue.

The sky was blue, but there a smoke
Hung still above the sea
Where the ships together spoke
To towns we could not see.

Could you have seen us through a glass
You would have said a walk
Of farmers out to turn the grass
Each with his own hay-fork.

The watchers in their leopard suits
Waited till it was time,
And aimed between the belt and boot
And let the barrel climb.

I must lie down at once, there is
A hammer at my knee.
And call it death or cowardice,
Don't count again on me.

Everything's alright, Mother,
Everyone gets the same
At one time or another.
It's all in the game.

I never strolled, nor ever shall,
Down such a leafy lane.
I never drank in a canal,
Nor ever shall again.

There is a whistling in the leaves
And it is not the wind,
The twigs are falling from the knives
That cut men to the ground.

Tell me, Master-Sergeant,
The way to turn and shoot.
But the Sergeant's silent
That taught me how to do it.

O Captain, show us quickly
Our place upon the map.
But the Captain's sickly
And taking a long nap.

Lieutenant, what's my duty,
My place in the platoon?
He too's a sleeping beauty,
Charmed by that strange tune.

Carentan O Carentan
Before we met with you
We never yet had lost a man
Or known what death could do.

LOUIS SIMPSON

NIGHT

But now the dark comes down cold, like a wet beast
Dropped on the dreaming floor of a farther and other
     night,
Terrible.
     Over the tundra the guns of the lost people,
The impatient ones, the midnight suicides,
Salute the war they have immoderately lost.

Fireworks in the rain ! And the dark circus . . .
Now the night-crawlers and the water-walkers
     appear :
Those who go home by sea to the ten-foot line;
And then the ingenious : swallowers of razor blades,
Truck drivers with ten feet of hose, the inventors
Who have found something high enough or strong
     enough to hang on;
And the shy loonies who can fall off cliffs.

Oh night ! Night ! In the nine hundred countries of
     the endless war
How cold you come: and sane ! John dear, dear
John Thomas what a burning in the snow there ! In
     the blank,
In the year-long dark, in the night when Raisin Jack
     is your sergeant —

(The squads in the boondack outposts tip-toeing
     down to the stills,
And the gone medics — crazy — the needles thick
     in their skins,
Adream in each others arms: the dying already
     dead
On their clean tables; and out in the storm the mad
Preachers calling curses into the rain) —

THOMAS McGRATH
From *Letter To An Imaginary Friend*

from ODE FOR THE AMERICAN DEAD IN KOREA

Wet in the windy countries of the dawn
The lone crow skirls his draggled passage home:
And God (whose sparrows fall aslant his gaze,
Like grace or confetti) blinks and he is gone,
And you are gone.   Your scarecrow valor grows
And rusts like early lilac while the rose
Blooms in Dakota and the stock exchange
Flowers. Roses, rents, all things conspire
To crown your death with wreaths of living fire.
And the public mourners come: the politic tear
Is cast in the Forum.   But, in another year,
We will mourn you, whose fossil courage fills
The limestone histories: brave: ignorant: amazed:
Dead in the rice paddies, dead on the nameless hills.

THOMAS MCGRATH

REARMAMENT

These grand and fatal movements toward death:
    the grandeur of the mass
Makes pity a fool, the tearing pity
For the atoms of the mass, the persons, the victims,
    makes it seem monstrous
To admire the tragic beauty they build.
It is beautiful as a river flowing or a slowly gathering
Glacier on a high mountain rock-face,
Bound to plow down a forest, or as frost in
    November,
The gold and flaming death-dance for leaves,
Or a girl in the night of her spent maidenhood,
    bleeding and kissing.
I would burn my right hand in a slow fire
To change the future . . . I should do foolishly.
    The beauty of modern
Man is not in the persons but in the
Disastrous rhythm, the heavy and mobile masses,
    the dance of the
Dream-led masses down the dark mountain.

ROBINSON JEFFERS

I WISH THE WOOD-CUTTER WOULD WAKE UP

And thou, Capernaum, which are exalted to heaven,
shalt be thrust down to hell . . . Luke, X, 15.

West of the Colorado River
there's a place I love.
I take refuge there with everything alive
in me, with everything
that I have been, that I am, that I believe in.
Some high red rocks are there, the wild
air with its thousand hands
has turned them into human buildings.
The blind scarlet rose from the depths
and changed in these rocks to copper, fire, and
        energy.
America spread out like a buffalo skin,
light and transparent night of galloping,
near your high places covered with stars
I drink down your cup of green dew.

Yes, through acrid Arizona and Wisconsin full of
        knots,
as far as Milwaukee, raised to keep back the wind
        and the snow
or in the burning swamps of West Palm,
near the pine trees of Tacoma, in the thick odor
of your forests which is like steel,
I walked weighing down the mother earth,
blue leaves, waterfalls of stones,
hurricanes vibrating as all music does,
rivers that muttered prayers like monasteries,
geese and apples, territories and waters,
infinite silence in which the wheat could be born.

I was able there, in my deep stony core, to stretch
          my eyes, ears, hands,
far out into the air until I heard
books, locomotives, snow, battles,
factories, cemeteries, footsteps, plants,
and the moon on a ship from Manhattan,
the song of the machine that is weaving,
the iron spoon that eats the earth,
the drill that strikes like a condor,
and everything that cuts, presses, runs, sews :
creatures and wheels repeating themselves and being
          born.
I love the farmer's small house. New mothers are
          asleep
With a good smell like the sap of the tamarind,
          clothes
just ironed. Fires are burning in a thousand homes,
with drying onions hung around the fireplace.
(When they are singing near the river the men's
voices are deep as the stones at the river bottom;
the tobacco rose from its wide leaves
and entered these houses like a spirit of the fire.)
Come deeper into Missouri, look at the cheese and
          the flour,
the boards aromatic and red as violins,
the man moving like a ship among the barley,
the blue-black colt just home from a ride smells
the odor of bread and alfalfa :
bells, poppies, blacksmith shops,
and in the rundown movies in the small towns,
love opens its mouth full of teeth
in a dream born of the earth.
What we love is your peace, not your mask.
Your warrior's face is not handsome.
North America, you are handsome and spacious.

You come, like a washerwoman, from
a simple cradle, near your rivers, pale.
Built up from the unknown,
what is sweet in you is your hive-like peace.
We love the man with his hands red
from the Oregon clay, your negro boy
who brought you the music born
in his country of tusks : we love
your city, your substance,
your light, your machines, the energy
of the West, the harmless
honey from hives and little towns,
the huge farmboy on his tractor,
the oats which you inherited
from Jefferson, the noisy wheel
that measures your oceanic earth,
the factory smoke and the kiss,
the thousandeth, of a new colony :
what we love is your workingman's blood :
your unpretentious hand covered with oil.
For years now under the prairie night
in a heavy silence on the buffalo skin
syllables have been asleep, poems
about what I was before I was born, what we were.
Melville is a sea fir, the curve of the keep
springs from his branches, an arm
of timber and ship. Whitman impossible to count
as grain, Poe in his mathematical
darkness, Dreiser, Wolfe,
fresh wounds of our own absence,
Lockridge more recently, all bound to the depths,
how many others, bound to the darkness :
over them the same dawn of the hemisphere burns,
and out of them what we are has come.

Powerful foot-soldiers, blind captains,
frightened at times among actions and leaves,
checked in their work by joy and by mourning,
under the plains crossed by traffic,
how many dead men in the fields never visited
          before;
innocent ones tortured, prophets only now published,
on the buffalo skin of the prairies.

From France, and Okinawa, and the atolls
of Leyte (Norman Mailer has written it out)
and the infuriated air and the waves,
almost all the men have come back now,
almost all . . . The history of mud and sweat
was green and sour; they did not hear
the singing of the reefs long enough
and perhaps never touched the islands, those wreaths
          of brilliance and perfume,
except to die :
                    dung and blood
hounded them, the filth and the rats,
and a fatigued and ruined heart that went on fighting.
But they have come back,
                    you have received them
into the immensity of the open lands
and they have closed (those who came back) like a
          flower
with thousands of nameless petals
to be reborn and forget.

PABLO NERUDA
translated by Robert Bly

AT THE BOMB TESTING SITE

At noon in the desert a panting lizard
waited for history, its elbows tense,
watching the curve of a particular road
as if something might happen.

It was looking at something farther off
than people could see, an important scene
acted in stone for little selves
at the flute end of consequences.

There was just a continent without much on it
under a sky that never cared less.
Ready for a change, the elbows waited.
The hands gripped hard on the desert.

WILLIAM STAFFORD

ON THE EVE

There is something sad about property
Where it ends, in California.

A patch of white is moving in a crack of the fence.
It is the rich widow.
When the dogs howl, she howls like a dog.

*

At night in San Francisco
The businessmen and drunkards
Sink down to the ocean floor.

Their lives are passing.
There is nothing in those depths
But the teeth of sharks and the earbones of whales.

Their lives are passing
Slowly under the scrutiny
Of goggle eyes, in waves that are vaguely

Connected to women.
The women stand up in cages
And do it, their breasts in yellow light.

The businessmen of San Francisco
Are mildly exhilarated.
Lifting their heavy arms and feet

They stamp on the ocean floor.
They rise from the ooze of the ocean floor
To the lights that float on the surface.

*

It is like night in St. Petersburg.
From the Bay a foghorn sounds,

And ships, wrapped in a mist,
Creep out with their heavy secrets
To the war "that no one wants."

LOUIS SIMPSON

56

THE PEOPLE

A CHRISTMAS NOTE FOR GERALDINE UDELL

Do the prairie flowers, the huge autumn
Moons, return in season?
Debs, Berkman, Larkin, Haywood, they are dead
    now.
All the girls are middle aged.
So much has escaped me, so much lies covert
In memory, and muffled
Like thunder muttering through sleep that woke me,
To watch the city wink
Out in the violet light under the twisting rain.
Lightning storms are rare here,
In this statistically perfect climate.
The eucalyptus shed
Branches, doors banged, glass broke, the sea
    smashed its walls.
I, in my narrow bed,
Thought of other times, the hope filled post war
    years,
Exultant, dishevelled
Festivals, exultant eyes, dishevelled lips,
Eyes dulled now, and lips thinned,
Festivals that have betrayed their occasions.
I think of you in *Gas*,
The heroine on the eve of explosion;
Or angry, white, and still,
Arguing with me about Sasha's tragic book.
Here in the empty night,
I light the lamp and hunt for pad and pencil.
A million sleepers turn,
While bombs fall in their dreams. The storm goes
    away,
Muttering in the hills.
The veering wind brings the cold, organic smell
Of the flowing ocean.

KENNETH REXROTH

THE PEOPLE

Wistful,
they speak of
satis-
faction, love

and divers
other
things. It
comforts,

it surprises
them, the
old
remembrances,

like hands to
hold them
safe and
warm. So

must it be, then,
some god looks
truly down
upon them.

ROBERT CREELEY

America the golden!
with trick and money
        damned
like Altgeld sick
        and molden
we love thee bitter
        land

Like Altgeld on the
        corner
seeing the mourners
        pass
we bow our heads
        before thee
and take our hats in
        hand

WILLIAM CARLOS WILLIAMS

"NIGHT HERE"

Night here,   a covert
All spun, webs in one
        how without grabbing hold it?
—Get into the bird-cage
        without starting them singing.

" Forming the New Society
        Within the shell of the Old "
The motto in the Wobbly Hall
Some old Finns and Swedes playing cards
Fourth and Yesler in Seattle.
O you modest, retiring, virtuous young ladies
        pick the watercress, pluck the yarrow
" Kwan kwan " goes the crane in the field,
        I'll meet you tomorrow;
A million workers dressed in black and buried,
We make love in leafy shade.

Bodhidharma sailing the Yangtze on a reed
Lenin in a sealed train through Germany
Hsuan Tsang, crossing the Pamirs
Joseph, Crazy Horse, living the last free
        starving high-country winter of their tribes.
Surrender into freedom, revolt into slavery—
Confucius no better—
        (with Lao-tzu to keep him in check)
" Walking about the countryside
        all one fall
To a heart's content beating on stumps."

GARY SNYDER

LOS ANGELES

They are herding our hearts down freeways.
The architects of America say
This is how it will be in another century:
We will join with armies of geese
In the cities of weeds,
Living on grass, in love with our own dung.

FLOYCE ALEXANDER

AMERICA

America I've given you all and now I'm nothing.
America two dollars and twentyseven cents
    January 17, 1956.
I can't stand on my own mind.
America when will we end the human war?
Go fuck yourself with your atom bomb.
I don't feel good don't bother me.
I won't write my poem till I'm in my right mind.
America when will you be angelic?
When will you take off your clothes?
When will you look at yourself through the grave?
When will you be worthy of your million
    Trotskyites?
America why are your libraries full of tears?
America when will you send your eggs to India?
I'm sick of your insane demands.
When can I go into the supermarket and buy what
    I need with my good looks?
America after all it is you and I who are perfect
    not the next world.
Your machinery is too much for me.
You made me want to be a saint.
There must be some other way to settle this argu-
    ment.
Burroughs is in Tangiers I don't think he'll come
    back it's sinister.
Are you being sinister or is this some form of
    practical joke?
I'm trying to come to the point.
I refuse to give up my obsession.
America stop pushing I know what I'm doing.
America the plum blossoms are falling.

I haven't read the newspapers for months, everyday
 somebody goes on trial for murder.
America I feel sentimental about the Wobblies.
America I used to be a communist when I was a
 kid I'm not sorry.
I smoke marijuana every chance I get.
I sit in my house for days on end and stare at the
 roses in the closet.
When I go to Chinatown I get drunk and never get
 laid.
My mind is made up there's going to be trouble.
You should have seen me reading Marx.
My psychoanalyst thinks I'm perfectly right.
I won't say the Lord's Prayer.
I have mystical visions and cosmic vibrations.
America I still haven't told you what you did to
 Uncle Max after he came over from Russia.
I'm addressing you.
Are you going to let your emotional life be run by
 Time Magazine?
I'm obsessed by Time Magazine.
I read it every week.
Its cover stares at me every time I slink past the
 corner candystore.
I read it in the basement of the Berkeley Public
 Library.
It's always telling me about responsibility. Business-
 men are serious. Movie producers are serious.
 Everybody's serious but me.
It occurs to me that I am America.
I am talking to myself again.

Asia is rising against me.
I haven't got a chinaman's chance.
I'd better consider my national resources.

My national resources consist of two joints of marijuana millions of genitals an unpublishable private literature that goes 1400 miles an hour and twentyfive-thousand mental institutions.

I say nothing about my prisons nor the millions of underprivileged who live in my flowerpots under the light of five hundred suns.

I have abolished the whorehouses of France, Tangiers is the next to go.

My ambition is to be President despite the fact that I'm a Catholic.

America how can I write a holy litany in your silly mood?

I will continue like Henry Ford my strophes are as individual as his automobiles more so they're all different sexes.

America I will sell you strophes $2500 apiece $500 down on your old strophe

America free Tom Mooney

America save the Spanish Loyalists

America Sacco & Vanzetti must not die

America I am the Scottsboro boys.

America when I was seven momma took me to Communist Cell meetings they sold me garbanzos a handful per ticket a ticket cost a nickel and the speeches were free everybody was angelic and sentimental about the workers it was all so sincere you have no idea what a good thing the party was in 1835 Scott Nearing was a grand old man a real mensch Mother Bloor made me cry I once saw Israel Amter plain. Everybody must have been a spy.

America you don't really want to go to war.

America it's them bad Russians.

Them Russians them Russians and them Chinamen.
    And them Russians.
The Russia wants to eat us alive. The Russia's
    power mad. She wants to take our cars from
    out our garages.
Her wants to grab Chicago. Her needs a Red
    Reader's Digest. Her wants our auto plants in
    Siberia. Him big bureaucracy running our
    fillingstations.
That no good. Ugh. Him made Indians learn read.
    Him need big black niggers. Hah. Her make
    us all work sixteen hours a day. Help.
America this is quite serious.
America this is the impression I get from looking
    in the television set.
America is this correct?
I'd better get right down to the job.
It's true I don't want to join the Army or turn
    lathes in precision parts factories, I'm near-
    sighted and psychopathic anyway.
America I'm putting my queer shoulder to the wheel.

ALLEN GINSBERG

AN IMITATOR OF BILLY SUNDAY

Billy Sunday, the frightening preacher, does not dare to come to this "city of heathens." However, he has disciples with a certain relative "power." One of these is Pastor A. Ray Petty, of the Anabaptist Church in Washington Square. Here are two of his public announcements:

Notice in " C "

THE CRISES OF THE CHRIST

Organ recital 7.45 P.M.
Preaching 8 P.M.

SPECIAL SUNDAY EVENING SERVICES

A. RAY PETTY

	APRIL	2nd	CHRIST AND THE CROWD
		9th	CHRIST AND THE COWARD
TOPICS		16th	CHRIST AND THE CROSS
		23rd	CHRIST AND THE CONQUEST
		30th	CHRIST AND THE CROWN

SPECIAL MUSIC — GOOD SINGING

YOU ARE WELCOME

BASEBALL SERMONS

SUNDAY EVENINGS AT 8 P.M.

A. RAY PETTY, PASTOR

	MAY 14th	THE PINCH HITTER
TOPICS	MAY 21st	THE SACRIFICE HIT
	MAY 28th	THE GAME CALLED ON ACCOUNT OF DARKNESS

LIVE MESSAGES   HOT OFF THE BAT

A spring night. Washington Square green, the sky still faintly gold from the day which was hot and dusty; the moon moves like a bird made of the light from tree to tree; the air is moist from jets of water whose tips are sheared off by the gusty and welcome wind. The Square looks like a tenement courtyard. Tumble-down people are asleep on the benches in a friendly forgiveness of each other. And drunks, drunks, drunks, talking to children, to the moon, to everyone going by. . . Bursts of music can be heard from MacDougal Alley, and voices of dancers from the houses with open doors. The church also stands wide open. Into it go the cries of the street children, and out of it come the cries of the half fear-inspiring pastor, who is throwing himself about now, his collar off, sweating and waving his arms, in his baseball sermon.

JUAN RAMÓN JIMÉNEZ
translated by Robert Bly

from DANCE OF DEATH

While the Chinaman was crying on the roof
without finding the nakedness of his wife,
and the bank president was watching the pressure-
     gage
that measures the ruthless silence of money,
the black mask was arriving at Wall Street.

This series of nitches whose eyes turn yellow
is not an odd place to dance in.
There is a wire stretched from the Sphinx to the
     safety deposit box
that passes through the heart of all the children
     who are poor.
The primitive energy is dancing with the machine
     energy,
in their frenzy totally ignorant of the original light.
Because if the wheel would forget its formula,
it would sing naked with the herds of horses;
and if a flame burns up the frozen budgets,
the sky will have to run away from the uproar of
     the windows.

This place is not an odd place for dancing, and
     I say this truth.
The black mask will dance between columns of
     numbers and blood,
among tornados of gold and groans of unemployed
     workers

who will go howling, dark night, through your time
    without lamps.
O savage North America! shameless! savage,
stretched out on the frontier of the snow!

The black mask! Look at the black mask!
What a wave of filth and glow-worms over New
    York!

FEDERICO GARCIA LORCA
translated by Robert Bly

THE UNITED STATES

America, you are luckier
Than this old continent of ours;
You have no ruined castles
And no volcanic earth.
You do not suffer
In hours of intensity
From futile memories
And pointless battles.

Concentrate on the present joyfully!
And when your children write books
May a good destiny keep them
From knight, robber, and ghost-stories.

GOETHE
translated by Robert Bly

THE MAN IN THE DEAD MACHINE

High on a slope in New Guinea
the Grumann Hellcat
lodges among bright vines
as thick as arms. In 1943
the clenched hand of a pilot
glided it here
where no one has ever been.

In the cockpit the helmeted
skeleton sits
upright, held
by dry sinews at neck
and shoulder, and webbing
that straps the pelvic cross
to the cracked
leather of the seat, and the breastbone
to the canvas cover
of the parachute.

Or say that the shrapnel
missed him, he flew
back to the carrier, and every
morning takes the train, his pale
hands on his black case, and sits
upright, held
by the firm webbing.

DONALD HALL

from A POEM BEGINNING WITH A LINE
BY PINDAR

Hoover, Roosevelt, Truman, Eisenhower—
where among these did the power reside
that moves the heart? What flower of the nation
bride-sweet broke to the whole rapture?
Hoover, Coolidge, Harding, Wilson,
hear the factories of human misery turning out
    commodities.
For whom are the holy matins of the heart ringing?
Noble men in the quiet of morning hear
Indians singing the continent's violent requiem.
Harding, Wilson, Taft, Roosevelt,
idiots fumbling at the bride's door,
hear the cries of men in meaningless debt and war.
Where among these did the spirit reside
that restores the land to productive order?
McKinley, Cleveland, Harrison, Arthur,
Garfield, Hayes, Grant, Johnson,
dwell in the roots of the heart's rancour.
How sad 'amid lanes and through old woods'
    echoes Whitman's love for Lincoln!

There is no continuity then. Only a few
    posts of the good remain. I too
that am a nation sustain the damage
    where smokes of continual ravage
obscure the flame.
             It is across great scars of wrong
    I reach toward the song of kindred men
    and strike again the naked string
old Whitman sang from. Glorious mistake!
    that cried :

74

'The theme is creative and has vista.'
'He is the president of regulation.'

   I see always the under-side turning,
fumes that injure the tender landscape.
   From which up break
lilac blossoms of courage in daily act
   striving to meet a natural measure.

ROBERT DUNCAN

AUTUMN BEGINS IN MARTINS FERRY, OHIO

In the Shreve High football stadium,
I think of Polacks nursing long beers in Tiltonsville,
And gray faces of Negroes in the blast furnace at
    Benwood,
And the ruptured night-watchman of Wheeling
    Steel,
Dreaming of heroes.

All the proud fathers are ashamed to go home.
Their women cluck like starved pullets,
Dying for love.

Therefore,
Their sons grow suicidally beautiful
At the beginning of October,
And gallop terribly against each other's bodies.

JAMES WRIGHT

THE AMBASSADORS

The dark and alien watch,
Winging to their cities,
The pale men with worried faces,

The men from the West:
That ruled, but now propose treaties;
That smile, but need time.

Flesh moves in huge landslides,
Overwhelming the Ambassadors
Even as they extend their hands.

WILLIAM BURFORD

We have made hawks
that fly
where no hawks have flown.

We have made hard sky
and look out at the rain.

We have made warm hides
from no animal yet slain.

We have made horses
that stride
as no horses ever known.

> *But, we are weak.*
> *On our wounded plains, we are alone.*

We have forgotten
the shape and cry of our bellies.

We have forgotten
the dances of our own faces,
the songs of our own voices.

We have forgotten
the chants of the souls
in our running feet.

> *Now, we remember.*
> *In our weeping tents, we are alone.*

GENE FOWLER

THE MOUTH OF THE HUDSON

(For Esther Brooks)

A single man stands like a bird-watcher,
and scuffles the pepper and salt snow
from a discarded, gray
Westinghouse Electric cable drum.
He cannot discover America by counting
the chains of condemned freight-trains
from thirty states. They jolt and jar
and junk in the siding below him.
He has trouble with his balance.
His eyes drop,
and he drifts with the wild ice
ticking seaward down the Hudson,
like the blank sides of a jig-saw puzzle.

The ice ticks seaward like a clock.
A Negro toasts
wheat-seeds over the coke-fumes
of a punctured barrel.
Chemical air
sweeps in from New Jersey.
and smells of coffee.

Across the river,
ledges of suburban factories tan
in the sulphur-yellow sun
of the unforgiveable landscape.

ROBERT LOWELL

NIGHT JOURNEY

Now as the train bears west,
Its rhythm rocks the earth,
And from my Pullman berth
I stare into the night
While others take their rest.
Bridges of iron lace,
A suddenness of trees,
A lap of mountain mist
All cross my line of sight,
Then a bleak wasted place,
And a lake below my knees.
Full on my neck I feel
'The straining at a curve;
My muscles move with steel,
I wake in every nerve.
I watch a beacon swing
From dark to blazing bright;
We thunder through ravines
And gullies washed with light.
Beyond the mountain pass
Mist deepens on the pane;
We rush into a rain
That rattles double glass.
Wheels shake the roadbed stone,
The pistons jerk and shove,
I stay up half the night
To see the land I love.

THEODORE ROETHKE

from THE RIVER

                    Behind
My father's cannery works I used to see
Rain-squatters ranged in nomad raillery,
The ancient men—wifeless or runaway
Hobo-trekkers that forever search
An empire wilderness of freight and rails.
Each seemed a child, like me, on a loose perch,
Holding to childhood like some termless play.
John, Jake or Charley, hopping the slow freight
—Memphis to Tallahassee—riding the rods,
Blind fists of nothing, humpty-dumpty clods.

Yet they touch something like a key perhaps.
From pole to pole across the hills, the states
—They know a body under the wide rain;
Youngsters with eyes like fjords, old reprobates
With racetrack jargon,—dotting immensity
They lurk across her, knowing her yonder breast
Snow-silvered, sumac-stained or smoky blue—
Is past the valley-sleepers, south or west.
—As I have trod the rumorous midnights, too,

And past the circuit of the lamp's thin flame
(O Nights that brought me to her body bare!)
Have dreamed beyond the print that bound her name.
Trains sounding the long blizzards out—I heard
Wail into distances I knew were hers.

Papooses crying on the wild's long mane
Screamed redskin dynasties that fled the brain,
—Dead echoes! But I knew her body there,
Time like a serpent down her shoulder, dark,
And space, an eaglet's wing, laid on her hair.

Under the Ozarks, domed by Iron Mountain,
The old gods of the rain lie wrapped in pools
Where eyeless fish curvet a sunken fountain
And re-descend with corn from querulous crows.
Such pilferings make up their timeless eatage,
Propitiate them for their timber torn
By iron, iron—always the iron dealt cleavage!
They doze now, below axe and powder horn.

And Pullman breakfasters glide glistening steel
From tunnel into field—iron strides the dew—
Straddles the hill, a dance of wheel on wheel.
You have a half-hour's wait at Siskiyou,
Or stay the night and take the next train through.
Southward, near Cairo passing, you can see
The Ohio merging,—borne down Tennessee;
And if it's summer and the sun's in dusk
Maybe the breeze will lift the River's musk
—As though the waters breathed that you might
    know
Memphis Johnny, Steamboat Bill, Missouri Joe.
Oh, lean from the window, if the train slows down,
As though you touched hands with some ancient
    clown,
—A little while gaze absently below
And hum *Deep River* with them while they go.

HART CRANE

THE DREAM

Someone approaches to say his life is ruined
and to fall down at your feet
and pound his head upon the sidewalk.
Blood spreads in a puddle.
And you, in a weak voice, plead
with those nearby for help;
your life takes on his desperation.
He keeps pounding his head.
It is you who are fated;
and you fall down beside him.
It is then you are awakened,
the body gone, the blood washed from the ground,
the stores lit up with their goods.

DAVID IGNATOW

SUNRISE

The Sunrise of New York
Has four columns of filth
And a hurricane of black pigeons
That putter in the putrid waters.

The sunrise of New York groans
Up the immense staircases
Searching on the edges for delicately sketched
Nardplants of anguish.

The sunrise arrives, and no one opens his mouth
      to receive it,
Because˙here the existence of tomorrow or hope
      is impossible.
Only now and then mad swarms of nickels and
      dimes
Sting and eat the abandoned children.

The first to leave their houses grasp in their bones
That there shall be no paradise nor love affairs
      without leaves;
They know they are going to the filth of numbers
      and laws,
To the games anyone can play, and the work that
      has no fruit.

The light is buried already by noises and chains
In the obscene threat of science that has no roots.
Through the suburbs people who cannot sleep are
      staggering
As though recently rescued from a shipwreck of
      blood.

FEDERICO GARCIA LORCA
translated by Robert Bly

ORIGINALS OF THE POEMS
IN GERMAN AND SPANISH

UN ALERTA PARA ABRAHAM LINCOLN

Mi capitán, yo he visto
cómo salen del hueco de tu herida
las abejas contentas,
a posarse en los ojos de Walt Whitman
y a mecerle la barba rumorosa.

Mi capitán, te busco
porque oí que te quieren asesinar de nuevo.
Y esta vez lo sabemos.

Oye las pisadas
de quien tras de la puerta conspira entre langostas,
suelta la nube y goza ya con el hartazgo de los verdes.

Alerta, capitán, alerta.
Que tiemblan las espigas y está sombrío el cielo.
Élitros y tenazas y mandíbulas
te están diciendo: alerta.

Allí, en tu palco.

Lo sé yo y te lo digo,
porque el eclipse anda rondando los campos más hermosos.
Y no quedará piedra sobre piedra,
porque ya tu ciudad está llorando por sus grietas.

Si te matan de nuevo,
quién sacará la miel de tus colmenas,
ni encauzará los trenes
de tu leche de paz a tus hormigas.

Si te matan de nuevo,
quién verá por tus hormigas negras.
Si te matan de nuevo,
ya nunca más será posible,
ni tan siquiera en el laurel del sueño,
la ronda de tus hormigueros
entre el sol y la noche.

Mi capitán, te busco
para decirte que te buscan
con la boca de la pistola
que ya quisiera abrirte la nueva herida sin abejas,
ay, porque en ese heuco de tu merte sin sangre
perecerían todas tus colmenas.

Y en dónde
pudiéramos entonces enterrarte
los que nos vamos por tu voz de abeja
a bebemos de tus ojos tristes.

En dónde,
que no fueras un vivo sino un muerto.

JACINTO FOMBONA-PACHANO.

A ROOSEVELT

1904

Es con voz de la Biblia o verso de Walt Whitman
que habría de llegar hasta ti, cazador.
Primitivo y moderno, sencillo y complicado,
con un algo de Wáshington y cuatro de Nemrod.
Eres los Estados Unidos,
eres el futuro invasor
de la América ingenua que tiene sangre indígena,
que aún reza a Jesucristo y aún habla en español.
Eres soberbio y fuerte ejemplar de tu raza;
eres culto, eres hábil; te opones a Tolstoi.
Y domando caballos o asesinando tigres,
eres un Alejandro-Nabuconodonosor.
(Eres un professor de energía,
como dicen los locos de hoy.)

Crees que la vida es incendio,
que el progreso es erupción,
que en donde pones la bala
el porvenir pones.

                    No.
Los Estados Unidos son potentes y grandes.
Cuando ellos se estremecen hay un hondo temblor
que pasa por las vértebras enormes de los Andes.
Si clamáis, se oye como el rugir del león.
Y Hugo a Grant le dijo: 'Las estrellas son vuestras'.
(Apenas brilla, alzándose, el argentino sol
y la estrella chilena se levanta . . .) Sois ricos.
Juntáis al culto de Hércules el culto de Mammón;
y alumbrando el camino de la fácil conquista,
la Libertad levanta su antorcha en Nueva York.

91

Mas la América nuestra, que tenía poetas
desde los viejos tiempos de Netzahualcoyotl,
que ha guardado las heullas de los pies del gran Baco,
que el alfabeto pánico en un tiempo aprendió;
que consultó los astros, que conoció la Atlántida
cuyo nombre nos llega resonando en Platón,
que desde los remotos mementos de su vida
vive de luz, de fuego, de perfume, de amor,
la América del grande Moctezuma, del inca,
la América fragrante de Cristóbal Colón,
la América católica, la America española,
la América en que dijo el noble Guatemoc:
'Yo no estoy en un lecho de rosas'; esa América
que tiembla de huracanes y que vive de Amor,
hombres de ojos sajones y alma bárbara, vive,
y sueña, y ama, y vibra, y es la hija del Sol.
Tened cuidado. ¡Vive la América española!
Hay mil cachorros sueltos del León español.
Se necesitaría, Roosevelt, ser por Dios mismo,
el Riflero terrible y el fuerte Cazador
para poder tenernos en vuestras férreas garras.

Y, pues contáis con todo, falta una cosa: ¡Dios!

RUBEN DARIO

LA UNITED FRUIT CO.

Cuando sonó la trompeta, estuvo
todo preparado en la tierra,
y Jehová repartió el mundo
a Coca-Cola Inc., Anaconda,
Ford Motors, y otras entidades:
la Compañía Frutera Inc.
se reservó lo más jugoso,
la costa central de mi tierra,
la dulce cintura de América.
Bautizó de nuevo sus tierras
como "Repúblicas Bananas,"
y sobre los muertos dormidos,
sobre los héroes inquietos
que conquistaron la grandeza,
la libertad y las banderas,
estableció la ópera bufa:
enajenó los albedríos,
regaló coronas de César,
desenvainó la envidia, atrajo
la dictadura de las moscas,
moscas Trujillos, moscas Tachos,
moscas Carías, moscas Martínez,
moscas Ubico, moscas húmedas
de sangre humilde y mermelada,
moscas borrachas que zumban
sobre las tumbas populares,
moscas de circo, sabias moscas
entendidas en tiranía.

Entre las moscas sanguinarias
la Frutera desembarca,
arrasando el café y las frutas,
en sus barcos que deslizaron
como bandejas el tesoro
de nestras tierras sumergidas.

Mientras tanto, por los abismos
azucarados de los puertos,
caían indios sepultados
en el vapor de la mañana:
un cuerpo rueda, una cosa
sin nombre, un número caído,
un racimo de fruta muerta
derramada en el pudridero.

PABLO NERUDA.

LOS DICTADORES

Ha quedado un olor entre los cañaverales:
una mezcla de sangre y cuerpo, un penetrante
pétalo nauseabundo.
Entre los cocoteros las tumbas están llenas
de huesos demolidos, de estertores callados.
El delicado sátrapa conversa
con copas, cuellos y cordones de oro.
El pequeño palacio brilla como un reloj
y las rápidas risas enguantadas
atraviesan a veces los pasillos
y se reúnen a las voces muertas
y a las bocas azules frescamente enterradas.
El llanto está escondido como una planta
cuya semilla cae sin cesar sobre el suelo
y hace crecer sin luz sus grandes hojas ciegas.
El odio se ha formado escama a escama,
golpe a golpe, en el agua terrible del pantano,
con un hocico lleno de légamo y silencio.

PABLO NERUDA.

QUE DESPIERTE EL LEÑADOR

*... Y tu Capharnaum, que hasta los
cielos estas levantada, hasta los infiernos
seras abajada. ...*

San Lucas, X, 15.

Al oeste de Colorado River
hay un sitio que amo.
Acudo allí con todo lo que palpitando
transcurre en mí, con todo
lo que fuí, lo que soy, lo que sostengo.
Hay unas altas piedras rojas, el aire
salvaje de mil manos
las hizo edificadas estructuras:
el escarlata ciego subió desde el abismo
y en ellas se hizo cobre, fuego y fuerza.
América extendida como la piel de búfalo,
aérea ya clara noche del galope,
allí hacia las alturas estrelladas,
bebo tu copa de verde rocío.

Sí, por agria Arizona y Wisconsin nudoso,
hasta Milwaukee levantada contra el viento y la nieve
o en los enardecidos pantanos de West Palm,
cerca de los pinares de Tacoma, en el espeso
olor de acero de tus bosques,
anduve pesando tierra madre,
hojas azules, piedras de cascada,
huracanes que temblaban como toda la música,
ríos que rezaban como los monasterios,
ánades y manzanas, tierras y aguas,
infinita quietud para que el trigo nazca.

Allí pude, en mi piedra central, entender al aire
ojos, oídos, manos, hasa oír
libros, locomotoras, nieve, luchas,
fábricas, tumbas, vegetales, pasos,
y de Manhattan la luna en el navío,
el canto de la máquina que hila,
la cuchara de hierro que come tierra,
la perforadora con su golpe de condor
y cuanto corta, oprime, corre, cose:
seres y ruedas repitendo y naciendo.

Amo el pequeño hogar del *farmer*. Recientes madres
     duermen
aromadas como el jarabe del tamarindo, las telas
recién plachadas. Arde
el fuego de mil hogares rodeados de cebollas.
(Los hombres cuando cantan cerca del río tienen
una voz ronca como las piedras del fondo:
el tabaco salió de sus anchas hojas
y como un duende del fuego llegó a estos hogares.)
Missouri adentro venid, mirad el queso y la harina,
las tablas colorosas, rojas como violines,
el hombre navegando la cebada,
el potro azul recién montado huele
el aroma del pan y de la alfalfa·
campanas, ampolas, herrerías,
y en los destartalados cinemas silvestres
el amor abre su dentadura
en el sueño nacido de la tierra.
Es tu paz lo que amamos, no tu máscara.
No es hermoso tu rostro de guerrero.
Eres hermosa y ancha Norte América.
Vienes de humilde cuna como una lavandera,
junto a tus ríos, blanca.
Edificada en lo desconocido,

es tu paz de panal lo dulce tuyo.
Amamos tu hombre con las manos rojas
de barro de Oregón, tu niño negro
que te trajo la música nacida
en su comarca de marfil: amamos
tu ciudad, tu substancia,
tu luz, tus mecanismos, la energía
del Oeste, la pacífica
miel, de colmenar y aldea,
el gigante muchacho en el tractor,
la avena que heredaste
de Jefferson, la rueda rumorosa
que mide tu terrestre oceanía,
el humo de una fábrica y el beso
número mil de una colonia nueva:
tu sangre labradora es la que amamos:
tu mano popular llena de aceite.

Bajo la noche de las praderas hace ya tiempo
reposan sobre la piel del búfalo en un grave
silencio las sílabas, el canto
de lo que fuí antes de ser, de lo que fuimos.
Melville es un abeto marino, de sus ramas
nace una curva de carena, un brazo
de madera y navío. Whitman innumerable
como los cereales, Poe en su matematica
tiniebla, Dreiser, Wolfe,
frescas heridas de nuestra propia ausencia,
Lockridge reciente, atados a la profundidad,
cuántos otros, atados a la sombra:
sobre ellos la misma aurora del hemisferio arde
y de ellos está hecho lo que somos.
Poderosos infantes, capitanes ciegos,
entre acontecimientos y follajes amedrentados a veces,
interrumpidos por la alegría y por el duelo,

bajo las praderas cruzadas de tráfico,
cuántas muertos en las llanuras antes no visitadas:
inocentes atormentados, profetas recién impresos,
sobre la piel del búfalo de läs praderas.

De Francia, de Okinawa, de los atolones
de Leyte (Norman Mailer lo ha dejado escrito),
del aire enfurecido y de las olas,
han regresado casi todos los muchachos.
Casi todos . . . Fué verde y amarga la historia
de barrio y sudor: no oyeron
bastante el canto de los arrecifes
ni tocaron tal vez sino para morir en las islas, las coronas
de fulgor y fragancia:
                      sangre y estiércol
los persiguieron, la mugre y las ratas,
y un cansado y desolado corazón que luchaba.
Pero ya han vuelto,
            los havéis recibido
en el ancho espacio de las tierras extendidas
y se han cerrado (los que han vuelto) como una corola
de innumerables pétalos anónimos
para renacer y olvidar.

Pablo Neruda.

from DANZA DE LA MUERTE

Cuando el chino lloraba en el tejado
sin encontrar el desnudo de su mujer
y el director del banco observaba el manómetro
que mide el cruel silencio de la moneda,
el mascarón llegaba al Wall Street.

No es extraño para la danza
este columbario que pone los ojos amarillos.
De la esfinge a la caja, de caudales hay un hilo tenso
que atraviesa el corazón de todos los niños pobres.
El ímpetu primitivo baila con el ímpetu mecánico,
ignorantes en su frenesí de la luz original.
Porque si la rueda olvida su fórmula,
ya puede cantar desnuda con las manadas de caballos;
y si una llama quema los helados proyectos,
el cielo tendrá que huir ante el tumulto de las ventanas.

No es extraño este sitio para la danza, yo lo digo.
El mascarón bailará entre columnas de sangre y de números,
entre huracanes de oro y gemidos de obreros parados
que aullarán, noche oscura, por tu tiempo sin luces,
¡oh salvaje Norteamérica! ¡oh impudica! ¡oh salvaje,
tendida en la frontera de la nieve!

El mascarón. ¡ Mirad el mascarón!
¡ Qué ola de fango y luciérnaga sobre Nueva York!

Federico Garcia Lorca.

UN IMITADOR
de Billy Sunday
New York.

Billy Sunday, el terrible predicador, no se atreve a venir a esta "Ciudad de incrédulos". Pero tiene discípulos de una "fuerza" relativa. Así este Pastor A. Ray Petty, de la Iglesia Anabaptista de Washington Square. He aquí dos de sus anuncios:

Anuncio en C:

THE CRISES OF THE CHRIST

Organ recital 7.45 P.M.
Preaching 8 P.M.

Special Sunday Evening Services

A. Ray Petty.

	April	2 d.	CHRIST AND THE CROWD
		9 th.	CHRIST AND THE COWARD
Topics		16 th.	CHRIST AND THE CROSS
		23 d.	CHRIST AND THE CONQUEST
		30 th.	CHRIST AND THE CROWN

Special Music—Good Singing
You Are Welcome

Es decir:

CRISIS DEL CRISTO

Recital de órgano a las 7.45 de la tarde,
Sermón a las 8 de la tarde.

Funciones Especiales El Domingo Por La Noche

A. Ray Petty.

	Abril	2	CRISTO Y LA CATERVA
		9	CRISTO Y EL COBARDE
Temas		16	CRISTO Y LA CRUZ
		23	CRISTO Y LA CONQUISTA
		30	CRISTO Y LA CORONA

Música Extraordinaria—Buen Canto
¡ Bienvenido Seas!

Anuncio en SPORTSMAN

Baseball Sermons

SUNDAY EVENING at 8 P.M.

A. Ray Petty, Pastor.

	May 14 th.	THE PINCH HITTER
Topics	MAY 21 st.	THE SACRIFICE HIT
	May 28 th.	GAME CALLED ON ACCOUNT OF DARKNESS

Live Messages   Hot Off The Bat

Es decir:

Sermones De Baseball

LOS DOMINGOS POR LA NOCHE, A LAS 8

A. Ray Petty, Pastor.

	Mayo 14	"EL PALA" EN APRIETO
Temas	Mayo 21	GOLPE SACRIFICADO
	Mayo 28	SE SUSPENDE EL JUEGO A CAUSA DE LA OSCURIDAD

Mensajes De Vida   Acabados De Salir De La Pala

. . . Es noche de primavera. La plaza, verde; el cielo, un poco dorado aún del día caliente y polvoriento; la luna, como un pájaro de luz, de árbol a árbol; el aire, húmedo de los surtidores desflecados por el viento fuerte y grato. Parece la plaza el gran patio de una casa de vecinos. En los bancos, jente sórdida, que duerme en fraternal desahogo. Borrachos, borrachos, borrachos hablando con niños, con la luna, con quien pasa. . . . De MacDougal Alley vienen musiquillas y gritos de la jente que se ve bailar en las casas abiertas. La iglesia tambien está de par en par. Entran en ella los gritos de los niños y salen de ella los gritos del pastor semiterrible que, sin cuello, se desgañita en su sermón— sudor y gesto—de frontón.

DEN VEREINIGTEN STAATEN

Amerika, du hast es besser
Als unser Kontinent, das alte,
Hast keine verfallene Schlösser
Und keine Basalte.
Dich stört nicht im Innern,
Zu lebendiger Zeit,
Unnützes Erinnern
Und vergeblicher Streit.

Benutzt die Gegenwart mit Glück!
Und wenn nun eure Kinder dichten,
Bewahre sie ein gut Geschick
Vor Ritter-, Räuber- und Gespenstergeschichten.

GOETHE.

LA AURORA

La aurora de Nueva York tiene
cuatro columnas de cieno
y un huracan de negras palomas
que chapotean las aguas podridas.

La aurora de Nueva York gime
por las inmensas escaleras
buscando entre las aristas
nardos de angustia dibujada.

La aurora llega y nadie la recibe en su boca
porque allí no hay manana ni esperanza posible.
A veces las monedas en enjambres uriosos
taladran y devoran abandonados ninos.

Los primeros que salen comprenden con sus huesos
que no habrá paraíso ni amore deshojados;
saben que van al cieno de números y leyes,
a los juegos sin arte, a sudores sin fruto.

La luz es sepultada por cadenas y ruidos
en impúdico reto de ciencia sin raíces.
Por los barrios hay gentes que vacilan insomnes
como recién salidas de un naufragio de sangre.

FEDERICO GARCIA LORCA.

ACKNOWLEDGMENTS

"Iowa, Kansas, Nebraska" by Gene Frumkin, Copyright © 1965 by Gene Frumkin, reprinted by permission of the author. "Eisenhower's Visit to Franco" and "Autumn Begins in Martins Ferry, Ohio" by James Wright, Copyright © 1962 by James Wright. Reprinted from *The Branch Will Not Break* by permission of Wesleyan University Press. "How Come" by David Ignatow, Copyright © 1960 by David Ignatow. Reprinted from *Say Pardon* by permission of Wesleyan University Press. "The Dream" by David Ignatow, reprinted from *Say Pardon* by permission of Wesleyan University Press. "I Know A Man" and "The People" are reprinted with the permission of Charles Scribner's Sons from *For Love* by Robert Creeley. Copyright © 1962 by Robert Creeley. "In the Oregon Country" and "At The Bomb Testing Site" by William Stafford, Copyright © 1960 by William Stafford, reprinted by permission of the author. "Canto LXXXIX" by Ezra Pound, *The Cantos (1-95)*. Copyright © 1956 by Ezra Pound. Reprinted by permission of New Directions Publishing Corporation. "A Warning to Abraham Lincoln" by Jacinto Fombona-Pachano. Copyright © 1940 by Jacinto Fombona-Pachano. "On American Island Wars" from "Ode on a Time of Hesitation" by William Vaughn Moody from *Selected Poems*, reprinted by permission of the Houghton Mifflin Company. Selections by Hart Crane from Complete Poems and Selected Letters and Prose of Hart Crane. Permission of LIVERIGHT, Publishers, New York. Copyright 1933, 1958, 1966 by Liveright Publishing Corp. "The Dictators" and "The United Fruit Co." by Pablo Neruda, Copyright 1950 by Pablo Neruda, and "I Wish The Wood-Cutter Would Wake Up" by Pablo Neruda, Copyright 1948 by Pablo Neruda, reprinted by permission of the author. Translations of Neruda poems by Robert Bly, Copyright © 1967 by The Sixties Press, reprinted by permission of The Sixties Press. "The Odor of Blood" and "Ode For The American Dead In Korea" from *Figures from a Double World* by Thomas McGrath, Copyright © 1955 by Thomas McGrath, "Night" from *Letter to an Imaginary Friend* by Thomas McGrath, Copyright © 1963 by Thomas McGrath, by permission of the Swallow Press. "Carentan O Carentan" by Louis Simpson, Copyright © 1959 by Louis Simpson. Reprinted from *A Dream of Governors* by Louis Simpson, by permission of Wesleyan University Press. "On The Eve" by Louis Simpson, Copyright © 1967 by The Sixties Press, reprinted from The Sixties (#9), by permission of The Sixties Press and Louis Simpson. "Rearmament" (*Solstice and Other Poems*) by Robinson Jeffers. Copyright 1935 and renewed 1962 by Donnan Jeffers and Garth Jeffers. Reprinted from *Selected Poetry of Robinson Jeffers*, by permission of Random House, Inc. "A Christmas Note for Geraldine Udell" by Kenneth Rexroth, *Collected Shorter Poems*. Copyright 1949 by Kenneth Rexroth, Reprinted by permission of New Directions Publishing Corporation. "America the Golden" from *Paterson* by William Carlos Williams. Copyright 1948 by William Carlos Williams. Reprinted by permission of New Directions Publishing Corpora-